Unmade Friend

Elegies

by

Peter Waldor

Finishing Line Press
Georgetown, Kentucky

Unmade Friend

Elegies

Also by Peter Waldor

Door to a Noisy Room
The Wilderness Poetry of Wu Xing
Who Touches Everything
The Unattended Harp
State of the Union
Gate Posts with No Gate
Nice Dumpling
Owl Gulch Elegies
Something About the Way

Publisher: Leah Huete de Maines
Editor: Christen Kincaid
Cover Art: Peter Waldor
Author Photo: Lisa Allee
Cover Design: Elizabeth Maines McCleavy

Order online: www.finishinglinepress.com
            also available on amazon.com

Author inquiries and mail orders:
Finishing Line Press
P. O. Box 1626
Georgetown, Kentucky 40324
U. S. A.

Table of Contents

In Memoriam…

Doctor David
Charlotte Fox
Bob Saunders

**Sign post
with no sign
Thank you
for giving
no direction**

I.

No More Humans

No more humans
but animals
keep an old
human trail intact
Their paws
drum the earth
The quadrupeds
are masters
of the elegy

Lanterns

Piles of fresh yellow
bear scat light my way
down the mountain
Past dusk I forgot
my light so thank god
for the dim fecal
lanterns keeping me
off cliff bands and slides
A passing thought
I could eat the berries
in the scat if I had to
A passing thought
I am closing
in on the beast
Every few yards
a fresh pile
Given the shapeliness
and luminescence
of the berries
buckthorn I think
it seems there was
very little digestion
not much help for
the looming hibernation

Common Sense

Common sense dictates
as I get deeper in wilderness
any trail will thin and vanish
leaving only animal paths, if that.
But I found a trail that
the further in—the further away
from civilization—the truer it becomes.
I still follow, though it goes
away from everything I know,
so remote even the lichens
converse without inhibitions
in their gravelly sopranos.

Extra Layers

A friend was found
near death,
hypothermic,
above Owl Gulch.
Her pack had pants,
hat, extra jackets,
an emergency blanket.
All stowed like an
axe in a glass case.
She had no explanation.

Old Climber

The fifth leg
of the spider's
eight legs
pressed the snow
and the avalanche
let go
Meanwhile
the old climber
was so slow
groaning up
the switchbacks
skis lashed to
her rucksack
she made it
for the aftermath
and not her burial
She lifted a shattered
pine branch to her face
and inhaled

King's Crown

How often must I
torture the poor
King's Crown flower

wilting in snow
with dreams of
monarchy's demise

The flower has
nothing to do
with its name

just as kings
don't ask
to be kings

Summertime
quiet down
see them

sporting their shaggy
crowns of pebbly maroon
blossoms cocked

sideways shaking
and gossiping with
the Penstemons

and the Elephant's Heads
of matters unrelated
to us

Last Dollar Saloon

A young climber
hoped to learn
others had died
on Lizard Head
before his climb
so when he
recounted it
at the Last Dollar
he could tell
the tragic history
and how the rock
fried away
every time he put
his weight on it

Shrine

Deep in wilderness
I found a shrine—
smooth stones on a dish.
The incense long since
blown and washed away.
Who carried that dish so high
and deep in the backcountry?
Must the supplicant be gone?
Can I never ask a question?

Brightness

All day in the wilderness
at night a squatter
in this lonely hut
I sweep with its broken broom
No carved initials scratched
into a rafter
Some shavings
a gut string and a file
perhaps a luthier
was last here
Moon brighter than sun
As much as I dream
of living with animals
I'll take the hard cot
and broken window

Aaron

When Aaron rolled down his window
on the lonely jeep road I had to accept
his invitation of guest friendship
so I climbed into his car
but I had trouble honoring to the letter
the biblical injunction for when he offered me
a beer I said no and when he offered me
a hit of acid I said no and when he
offered to take my name and address
to send me pictures of his cabin
hidden away in Owl Gulch and pictures of Chaco
that prove its extraterrestrial design
I said no but still we talked in a friendly manner
I didn't tell him that I once found
his hidden cabin and there was a note
he left on a paper plate wedged in the door
telling Woodsy Pauli there was kindling
apples and a blanket under a board
and whether it was right or not I don't know
but I did remind him that he yelled at me
a year ago on the same road when I was being
too noisy and he smiled and remembered
everything we both said that day
I am not sure he apologized but his memory
was apology enough and he said that
it was brave of me to get in the car
and I said what are you going to do
chop my head off and he smiled and reached
into the back and pulled out a machete
and put it on my lap and said he could
use this and I tested the blade
in a ceremonial manner with my thumb
it was so dull it was hard to believe
it ever could have been sharp
I reached for the door and there was
just a stub where the handle once was
Then he told me he was a student

of mental illness and chronicled
two or three examples in detail
It reminded me of my theory that all
students of the mind are crazy
or at least a little so
Finally Aaron reached across me
and with a deft jiggle opened the door
a good thing for me since my mother
is no Parvati who could simply rouse
the creatures of the wild and find
a volunteer to give me a fresh head
and I walked away the red rocks
of the canyon and the red dust
of the road all blanched
gray by the long dusk

Finally Turning Back

but taking
a mental picture
of where to go
next time
deeper into the wild
today noting an aspen
with barbed-wire
buried under
a thick-lipped scar
each time
further until
I bring that image
to my grave
where it will
be proudly displayed
in the great
Earth album

Distant avalanche

Drying sheets whipping in the wind

Tracks go wrong

Those who follow

lose their way

Saint Phocas the Gardener

What a fool waiting
until I was old
to go into the wild
with only a loincloth.
Today I got caught
in hail snow and rain,
no poncho or kindling pouch,
and then birdsong
at the storm's end.

Old when I lay naked
on mother earth.
If only I were young
the first time
I lay down like this
so now I would be laying
with an old friend,

in her twigs, needles, lichens
and dirt, the self-same dirt
Phocas dug through
carefully as a surgeon
so he wouldn't disturb
the roots in his garden.
We revere him for his
tranquility but tell me
he wasn't shaking.

Little Lithodendron Wash

Small coral branch
found by accident
by one searching
for something else
and so the name
on the topographic map
Gravel where there
was once water
mountains where
there was once sea
stardust where there was
something I don't
know the name of
On the map
the delineating lines
are like brushed hair
And one terribly
lonely man
in the wild simply
seeks more loneliness

Petroglyph

After a thousand years
an old ones's etching
crumbled off an overhang
into a powdery pile
There is a coyote's
paw print in the mound
on the cave floor
Some of the dust
stuck briefly to the paw
shaking off on the
creature's bright circuit

Test

With all the world's problems
I take a man
into the wilderness
to see if he notices
wildflowers
Even if he is kind
a good father
and helper of the poor
if he does not make genuine
frequent exclamations
ask questions
and try to learn
a name or two
I will never
talk to him again
He had three chances
with monkshood
which by the way
are most careful
listeners
in their purple hoods
drenched in venom

Early Winter

The bright yellow
bedraggled petals
of an "invasive"
the last blossoms
above Bridal Veil
How fitting
the invader is
the only survivor

Kiss of Death

Back at tree line a wolf
hops to and fro
like a child at the end
of a pier.
My climbing partner,
as usual, way ahead,
tinkling up the talus
like a pianist.
Not long enough
since she tried to take
her own life but just
missed that dark kiss.
What if the scree slides?
What if she falls
off the ridge?
What if this sacred mountain
has nothing to do
with healing suffering?
What if she didn't love Edith Piaf?
At least, on top,
she was breathing hard.
She squeezed my arm.
At least she signed
the summit register
in her Cyrillic style script
and left a goofy line
from Lao Tzu, something
about governing being
like frying small fish.
O dear hazards
of friendship!

Elegy for Glider Bob

1.
The day after he died, my son and I biked
near the crash site, high up, we stopped to rest
and in a hail storm found a patch of chanterelles,
the mother lode, we harvested in somber glee,
as I had unwanted thoughts about the cycle
of life and decomposition.

2.
Just through the clearing Bob's plane
was strapped to a flatbed truck,
minus wings, the fuselage was intact,
no crumpling near the cockpit.
It was a trespass to see the wreck.

3.
For all those years I thought I would wait
until I had a terminal illness, to give Bob
some glider business, but I had changed
my mind and was about to sign up.
After all, he had been gliding for 34 years.

4.
Four times I remember being on a peak
and Bob buzzing us, *buzz* is the wrong word,
whispered. I remember him smiling and waving.
That's a lie, but he did tilt a wing.

5.
Before the last town council election there was
a banner in front of the market "Anyone but Bob!"
What a credit to his vision, to inspire critics so.

6.
May 1, 2001, Bob played Mr. Cellophane
in a town park production of Chicago
during an epic hail storm and no one left.

7.
Who knew Bob made children's furniture?
His old friend took a mortised spindle
that Bob discarded. Now it's leaning
on the friend's wall. It is not needed
 to remind him of Bob. It will stay
there until his own time to go.

8.
Bob rode his hulking antique chrome Harley
with laughing finesse in the July fourth parade,
stars and stripes painted on head and face.
He fought for affordable housing.

9.
Fly quietly.
Unmade friend.

II.

Orphan Camel Colt

A good friend
of the missing climber
didn't volunteer with
Search and Rescue
and their eighty
person team sweeping
the scree and forest
Instead she searched
on her own ever higher
All she found above
Owl Gulch was an
orphan camel colt
no brand braid or bell
its humps sagging

Painted Ladies

Two painted ladies
make love
on and above
some moss and phlox
wings folded
together folded
and unfolded
like a knot tied
and untied
tied untied
rising tumbling
What would
they say if they
were forced to use
our rudimentary
language to describe
their passion
Is it like
a knife crossing
a whetstone
Ecstatic with the
pleasure of love
Yes love
Wings frayed from
the rough action
One knocks off
a white phlox petal
onto the emerald
moss mattress
The rest of the world
distant
as a butterfly's
forgotten dream

Gleaming Spiral

I stumbled on a cabin
in the wilderness
no one there
the door ajar
just a cot and potbelly stove
and tacked
to the pine board
a page torn from
a spiral notebook
the top frayed
A simple charcoal drawing
the charcoal
could have been lifted
right out of the stove
just a few lines
lovers
one on her back
and one prone above
man or woman
hard to say
The prone one's head
in the crotch of the
woman laying down
with her legs spread
halfway apart
feet curved down
like eyelashes
and her hands
are in the hair
of her lover
not quite holding
him or her in place
more a quiet gratitude
The fingers getting
lost in the hair
just lines really
quick strokes

and the paper itself
is warped as if
it had been jostled
after being torn from
the gleaming spiral
I fear it has been
crumpled and used
as kindling on
a cold night
the lovers going up
in flames as they
always do
the art
vanishing as it
always does

Fairies

Of course the fairies
weren't home when I found
their cabin with
a wicker outdoor table
and four pink doilies
the size of a child's
thumb nail
The great yellow
aspen leaves
floated down to bury
their homestead
If only mother and father
time could do away
with humanity in such
a gentle manner
but the old couple
don't even have
any background music
when they work
just the sound of their
blunt instruments which
are not my grandmother's
rolling pins

Green Gentian Stalk

Not easy for
a flower to give
birth to a flower
Brittle ruin
dead but erect
after waiting
seventy years
to bloom
Seeds trapped
in seed cases
dice in a casino cup

Hidden Sign

Blue bells
just buds
unnoticed

going up
the mountain
blossoms
going down

A steel sign
at the Deer Tail
Basin and Ballard

Mountain Trail
junction
Two drooping
rusty arrows

Deer Tail left Ballard right
How fanciful
to hide

a marker where
so few go
Blue bells
just buds

The popping
of the welder's torch
talus sliding

The welder
took big risks
in the mountains
Once he evaded

park rangers

and made a first
free ascent

at Shiprock
Then he died
of a disease
The arrows at

the end of the sign
could be drooping
hands on a cross

It was a good job
in the empire
to harvest oak
for crosses

in the dense
Massimina Forest
The woodsmen pair

could spend
tranquil days
above Rome
with their

two man saw
Blossoms
going down

Orpheus and Eurydice

The first time I walked
barefoot I took my boots
off to cross a river

and was too tired
to put them back on
so I climbed the mountain

barefoot not tired enough
to turn around just too tired
to put my boots back on

Once at the same crossing
my son turned back to look
at me and slipped all the way

into the water and I made
him continue though soaked
If only Orpheus slipped

as he started to turn
Maybe he wouldn't have
tried to turn again

after he picked himself up
and would have made it
out of hell with his love

Boset's Cut

Some men spend
their lives trying not
to be tired and others
do whatever they

can to wear
themselves out.
Boset is one of them,
shouldering his

chain saw
high up in Owl Gulch
with only flip flops
and patented black

silk gym shorts.
He cuts and rolls
logs away clearing
an unmarked trail.

He said it was so
his young niece
could walk the trail
without getting hurt

and when I told
his story to the
old mayor she said
he should be arrested.

Bad Sign

I suppose it's a bad sign
to sing the same
song again and again
and not realize I was

repeating it just thinking
it got more beautiful
I was carrying an old friend's
letter all the way up

to Porphyry Basin
Our friendship so old
her handwriting went
from elegant to jagged

A snowy field of bistorts
and the quartz debris
the rock hounds left behind
is fit for a shaman

I sit on a ledge and read
like a census taker who
lost his notebook and decided
he'll say he worked all day

Great Child

I met a young boy on a trail
Naturally I stopped to tell him
the name of a flower
It was a fairy trumpet
and by luck weeks later
I passed the same boy
with his parents and there
was a fairy trumpet and I
asked him its name and he
paused and grimaced and
he blurted out *pixie horn*

Splayed Cairns

A ranger friend
was fired when
the Forest Service
discovered she was
scattering trail cairns
in the wilderness.
They didn't understand
her kindness and how
she only wanted to help
us to find our own way.
You may find her high up,
with no water gourd,
her poncho
smelling of smoke,
her head
an eternal flame.
If you get lucky
she may stop to talk
about the weather.

Hermit

He finds foot prints deep
in the wilderness where he
thought he was the only one
and is joyful that there is
another hermit going
his own way until he
realizes it is only his own
footprints and he will never
meet anyone to discuss
how he carries water
or shelters or how
he can't go back

Lines

Tree line
Flower line
Rock line
Bird line
Sky line
Line in
the sand
Don't let wind
or rain
or enemies
obliterate it
Rather use
your strength
of mind

A La Junta Chute Avalanche

No humans perished
so no news articles
but notice the old growth

firs halved thirty feet
up their trunks and all
their skin abraded

Ten thousand flying hatchets
No—beyond count
Usnea on the ground

like cuttings on a barber
shop floor and the creek
vanished in the debris

High Pressure Vessel

On a lark on a day off
and with no governmental approvals
Kroger and a partner broke
a new trail above Tomboy Road
and they fixed three steel
markers in the branches
of some young aspens

Over the years since
he passed away the markers
have risen higher and higher
as the aspens matured
lifting them like a curtain
going up on a stage

the only sound
hemp ropes sliding over
pullies as the purple
velvet vanishes
into the proscenium

Of course there is
no stage no actors
and no audience
just a janitor
named Dandalia Morales
sweeping the auditorium

with her wide broom
before she goes downstairs
to monitor the boiler
and take a break
on a folding chair reading
a Pacaya Guatemala daily

happy next to her
high pressure vessel

but dreaming of walking
in her rope sandals
up Cerro la Serra
Kroger's partner who handed
the rivets up to him
to fix the signs
is an old man now
but still trudges the trail
and can't find the markers
when he looks up
into the canopy

Sometimes he crawls
on the snowdrifts
with his titanium hips
Last time he noticed
a pot belly stove left

from the mining days
had been taken
by a treasure hunter
and he was upset
the wilderness was
a little more wild

Elegy for Charlotte Fox

1
The secret to extreme mountain exploration
is to suffer unduly and then to feel
better even as conditions worsen.
Charlotte mastered this art.

2
Describing difficult moments, she would simply
say she helped out and was helped.

3
Given her 8,000-meter resume
it was hard to say hello when
our paths' crossed on Tomboy Road.
Did fame make her lonely?

4
Charlotte was private as a marmot,
but at base camps she would treat
the whole expedition to local brews,
and if you pulled her aside she'd
listen patiently to your story.

5
Her brief essay on the Everest climb
was a reproof to the best seller.
She said, in essence, Everest
is a sport climb for rich tourists,
mistakes were made, people died,
there is nothing more to say,
so don't say anything.

6
Someone pinned a sprig of lilac
between wiper and windshield
on her giant red expedition van.
Some will know why it is there.

Others will wonder why,
and some won't notice a thing
before her distant family
takes the van away.

III.

Sour Dough Starter

A favorite aunt cleaned
her fridge after the accident
keeping the Dijon and Coke
not noticing the white jar
of sour dough starter
blending in with the door
passed down 400 years
200 in Holland 200
in the "new" world
Once she baked loaves
for her friends after
a day of jam cracks
at Indian Creek
What will the new tenant
make of the jar
in the empty fridge
Will they do what
I would and toss it
quickly or will they recognize
its old bandage stink
and honor the tradition

Owl Gulch

Coyote pack racing
through the forest
a gray rain
blown sideways
Shimmer of
herring bone coats
I frantically search
the floor for a club
but they are not
looking for me
just marmots
or magpies
or a stray dog
unless they choose
to play with it instead

Death Rope

We called it the *death rope*
Orange with black flecks
160-meter Edelweiss
The proper thing
was to bury it
the way Jews bury
their scrolls if they
touch the ground
But years later in the Gunks
I drape it over my shoulder
taking the approach
in silence past the
no trespassing sign
and the condor nest
We may have laughed
nervously when we first
coiled it remembering
the accident
There will always be
the sounds of his
parents' howl and the
ringing of the poorly
placed piton falling
with the sandy haired
young man

Volunteers

Beautiful day and the eighty odd
search and rescue volunteers
were sweeping a new section
of forest fifty feet apart but
meeting frequently and talking
of many things some feeling
guilty for the glee they felt being
out in the summer wilderness
Since so many days had passed
and still no sign
the rumors were wild
a few were saying
it was a life insurance scam
and the lost one was relaxing
on a beach in Mexico
where their partner would
join them someday when
they were forgotten
and others said they were
on the same beach
with another lover
but I believed the talk
that they were killed
and dragged to a cave
by a mountain lion
so we couldn't find the body
though it would be better
for the children if they were
still alive even under
suspicious circumstances
And when the search party
dwindled to a few old friends
an airplane finally saw the body
just outside the search zone
When they reached the remains
they found a glass jar
of pine patch salve cracked

the salve dripping on the scree
Who knows if anyone felt
ashamed for talk of lovers
and life insurance
Do they hang their heads
passing the partner on Main Street
Are they disappointed
the lost one died doing
what they loved

The Hands of a Leper

He wasn't authentic
He came late
to the mountains
from a suburb of one
of the eastern cities
where he left his invalid
brother to take care
of his invalid mother
but he did get lost
and found many times
and late in life
he was afraid
even to touch trees
for he thought he had
the hands of a leper

Necessary Existence

On a giant snowfield
I saw a creature
settle down
onto the crystals
its rapid wings
invisible to
my human eyes
Smaller than a tick
bigger than dust
It was oval
or barrel shaped
and all I could
think of
was a whale
descending

Teacher

He died in an avalanche
while teaching
avalanche awareness
When he coiled
his black rope
if it ended in 23 coils
he flaked it apart
and started over
Once he confided
that although he loved
his loved ones
he loved most
of all the feeling
when he left them
and he was alone
reflecting on their
time together
driving west
all his gear
in his truck
with its weak lights
and rusted carriage
heading to Indian Creek
where a climber can
slip all the way
into a crack
like a flower
between pages

Old Climber

Once with an old climber
who had the trail memorized
and knew pretty much everything
about everything,
even telling me how pine trees
make many cones in times of stress,
we lost our way and when
I returned to the same mountain pass, alone,
I found the switchback we had missed.
Better to be a novice, but dangerous to be
smug about the advantage.

Cat's Paw Print

A cat paw print
on top a boot print
in the snow
no house cat
a mountain lion
I doubt the cat was
tracking the human
just taking an easy
way in a hard winter
There is a thin line
slashed from the edge
of the crater by a claw
that didn't quite
clear the powder
and a shadow
catching in the gouge
Speaking of predator
prey and prayer
surely all prayer
is predatory

The Royal's Heart

Early spring day
Fresh tongues of mud
roll across the snow
Marsh marigolds
unfurling and king's crowns
green fists poke through
We must say
the royal's heart
is no different
than anyone's
We must say it
to ourselves
to friends
to enemies
in our lover's ear
to the mud and snow
No difference

Notorious B.I.G.

In deep snow I follow
a confluence of elk tracks
not to find them and kill

one and not even
to find their secret place
They go their own way

I sit on a downed spruce
and weep for B.I.G.'s wife
punching 911 in her beeper

just before she was shot
and weep for B.I.G. racing
to her and when he saw

the ring of police he threw
his burner phone in the bushes
and made a U turn

Texas A & M

It's easy to be frightened in the wilderness
so when we saw the two from a distance
I thought the worst, kidnappers, or worse,
one held a large object and when we got
down from the ridge to the lake we met
and talked, they were geology grad students
from Texas A & M. He studied landslides
and the large object was a measuring rod
that extended to 16 feet, she studied water
and used his rod to measure depth and width
of drainages. He had a notebook with colored
sketches of slides. The quartz we found in
mining tailings did not impress them.
Though they were both heavy and dressed
in the floppy adventure clothes of city
people dressed for adventure, there was
something solemn and peaceful about them,
as if they were not living in our time
but a time when they could watch glaciers
flow, could see the earth spinning,
and mountains rise and fall like sand castles,
and we wanted to grill them about
their work but felt like we were intruding.
They descended and we were alone
again in the wilderness.
The earth is a drum and a mallet.
We are drum and mallet.
We waited for daylight to vanish
and the stars to fill up the heavens,
not knowing any names.
My son slept soundly and did not
hear the spray of rain on the tent fly
or the coyotes just outside the tent
celebrating a kill cackling like crones.
In the morning we broke camp quietly
and hiked down trying to notice
the shape of the land for the first time.

Air Forces

A man can kill many times
but can only be killed once
If only it were the reverse
If only we couldn't kill even once
And speaking of the great
beauty of warplanes
that break the silence of even
the most remote wilderness
parasailers are just as beautiful
If only the air forces
of the world limited themselves
to parasailing so there must
be a mountain next to
the enemy and a wind across
the border and little
capacity for bombs and leaflets

Three People

Three people walk
a ridge line
absent minded
as any bipeds
They get tapped
on shoulders
One gets a hug
and kiss one gets
a knife between
the ribs
the third just
keeps clamoring
on the brittle
white cornice

Shadow

I stumbled upon a hermit sitting
cross-legged in the wilderness,
weeping. I asked, why, not sure
I should say anything.
He said his shadow had inadvertently
crossed over a flower,
a ruby-throated penstemon,
and so it lost a moment's sun.
I moved on afraid my own
shadow crossed his light.

Two Rings

At tree line she passed
an aspen with two sets
of claw marks going up
from the base of the trunk,
one animal presumably
hunting another.
The razor slashes in the bark
long since scarred into bulbous
crescents—no telling if prey
evaded predator.
She touches both sets of scars
and smells her fingers.
Higher up in the frigid expanse
her fingers shrink a little
and her two rings,
one from her dead husband
one from her divorce,
clink like a cowbell
just at the edge of hearing.
She doesn't realize
it's her rings, but thinks
it really is a distant cowbell,
the sound carried up
from a pasture by a thermal.
She half dreams she was
laying on a porch beside
that pasture and half dreams
how happy she is far away
from human endeavors,
even their captive animals.

Old Married Couple

Every other day or so
walking the hard way
up Tomboy Road to the
long decommissioned
Savage Basin mines,
skins leathered
beautifully by lifetimes
above tree lines.
The chorus line of old legs.
Talking or not talking.
If you corner them
she won't say a thing
and he cheerfully
won't say much.
He won't say how
he lost his right arm,
one safety pin holding
the starched sleeve of his
rancher holiday shirt.
Seasons already
since we met
on the miners' road,
just a coincidence
the seep by
the big turn is dry now
even in spring.

Elegy for Doctor David

1
Nothing lives long
Nothing lives long
Nothing lives long
Not even the mountains,
chanted David's friends
at his cave.

2
Chanted White Antelope before
his murder at Sand Creek.

3
David had no money but
rented the Sheridan Opera House
for $500 and for twenty minutes,
in his silk wizard robe recited
his silent poem, long before
composers celebrated silence.

4
Who doesn't have a son with long hair?
When Absalom stole David's concubines
and declared himself King, he was undone
when his hair caught in a branch.
We would call it a bouffant, and while stuck
he was killed with three darts to his heart.

5
Wise move for David to leave Baltimore
and sojourn in Bear Creek where
his dreads grayed to his waist
and bears in nearby caves
never bothered him as he
practiced spirit healing.

6
Great caves are hard to enter
and hard to leave. David's friends
clawed up the cliffs to his cave
where he surveyed the wild
from his loam balcony.
His mattress, stove pipe, and healing
stones were all gone, just David's
silent poem and White Antelope's song.

7
White Antelope said the earth and the
mountains remain but David's friends
said they also don't last.

8
How irate David was when someone
called him "Black David" in his presence.

9
David never wrestled angels,
just walked barefoot with Mother Earth
and changed his name to Michal.

10
He was the Rainbow Gathering's
official healer, though they
abhor officials.
He drove their bus up Bear Creek
before the land was preserved and an
iron bar placed across the access trail.

11
David was inconsolable after Absalom's death
and hid in a cave where people found
him and begged him to return.

12
Just four or five people that night at the Sheridan.
David also had a radio show and once,
for an hour, played the sound of old shoes
walking down old stairs.

13
A friend of David's lost $500 in the wilderness
and though it was years later was it the $500
David used to rent the Sheridan.

14
David, your passing leaves us with no healer,
and White Antelope's children aren't
with us to chant against injustice.

15
At first, during the twenty-minute
silent poem the audience
fidgeted and sighed,
but then relaxed as if
a great weight was gone
though the weight of the world
was still there.

Peter **Waldor** is the author of eight books of poetry, including *Door to a Noisy Room* which won the Kinereth Gensler Award from Alice James Books, *Who Touches Everything*, which won the National Jewish Book Award and *Gate Posts with No Gate* which, is a collaboration with a group of visual artists. Waldor was the Poet Laureate of San Miguel County, Colorado from 2014 to 2015. His work has appeared in many journals, including the *American Poetry Review, Ploughshares, the Iowa Review, the Colorado Review, Poetry Daily, Verse Daily, Fungi Magazine* and *Mothering Magazine.* He lives in Telluride, Colorado.

www.ingramcontent.com/pod-product-compliance
Lightning Source LLC
Chambersburg PA
CBHW021156090426
42740CB00008B/1123